BLACK NATIVITY
MUSIC FROM THE MOTION PICTURE

ISBN 978-1-4803-6709-8

HAL•LEONARD®
CORPORATION

7777 W. BLUEMOUND RD. P.O. BOX 13819 MILWAUKEE, WI 53213

Visit Hal Leonard Online at
www.halleonard.com

BE GRATEFUL

Words and Music by
WALTER HAWKINS

*Recorded a half step lower.

COLDEST TOWN

Words and Music by RAPHAEL SAADIQ,
TAURA STINSON and KASI LEMMONS

TEST OF FAITH

Words and Music by RAPHAEL SAADIQ
and TAURA STINSON

A(add2)

ba - by, I'll be _____ home. _____

Bm7　　　　　　　　　　　　　Em

Hush, lit - tle ba - by, don't cry.

A(add2)　　　　　　　　　　　F#m11

You'll un - der - stand in, in due time.

Bm7　　　　　　　　　　　　　Em

Hush, lit - tle ba - by, don't say a thing;

MOTHERLESS CHILD

Traditional
Lyrics by RAPHAEL SAADIQ,
TAURA STINSON and H. DOOBIE POWELL
Arrangement by RAPHAEL SAADIQ and TAURA STINSON

*Recorded a half step lower.

Additional lyrics

Can't she see it breaks my heart to let her hug me?
Tell me, how can she send me away if she really loved me?
Been me and her since I set foot on this earth.
My daddy went M.I.A. after my birth.

Every time I look at my mama, I see her dilemma.
I'm the one thing standing between her and being a winner.
And she says, "How can I ever get it together when you be wilding out?"
Sometimes I feel like a motherless child, no doubt.

HUSH CHILD
(Get You Through the Silent Night)

Lyrics by TAURA STINSON
Music by KASI LEMMONS and TAYLOR GORDON

*Recorded a half step lower.

Home - less chil - dren with frost - bit - ten toes, Frost - bit - ten toes,

...- ing in the _____ street, _____
sleep - ing in the _____ street, _____

sleep - ing in _____ the street.
sleep - ing in _____ the street.

Male I (sung): The __ in - dif -

Male II (spoken):
I ain't tryin' to be philosophical, but it's not logical: Some folks out here freezin'; others chillin' like it's tropical.

G5   Fmaj7

-in'?   Get read-y for the wel-fare   line._____   I

Dm   Am   Bdim/A   Am

ain't tryin' to hear it.   You make the bed; lay in it,   but I'm way too strong for you to break my ____ spir-

N.C.

it.   Am I the cause of all ____ my moth-er's mis-er-y?   This cloud of se-cre-
Male II: Is   it   me?

cy   on my pa-ter-ni-ty,   Did my ver-y birth___ de-stroy__ my whole fam-i-ly?

vic - tion no - tice, but my Lord_ don't hear_ my_ prayers._ I've nev - er been_

_ this scared. The si - lence is _ too loud_ for me: _

that just ain't fair! _ Is an - y - one out _ there? (Does an - y - one care?) Is

Male I: *Female:*
an - y - one list - 'ning? (Is an - y - one there?) Just let me know that I'm a part of your plan and that

HE LOVES ME STILL

Words and Music by RAPHAEL SAADIQ,
TAURA STINSON and DARIEN DORSEY

CAN'T STOP PRAISING HIS NAME

Words and Music by RICKEY GRUNDY
and HERMAN NETTER
Additional Lyrics by TAURA STINSON

*Recorded a half step lower.

56

SWEET LITTLE JESUS BOY

Words and Music by
ROBERT MacGIMSEY

*Recorded a half step lower.

RISE UP SHEPHERD AND FOLLOW

Traditional
Arranged by RAPHAEL SAADIQ,
TAURA STINSON and H. DOOBIE POWELL

Rap Lyrics

Yeah, I'm the noble one, Obi-wan Kenobi one
Drunk my sweet and sober tongue about the Holy One.
Spread the word, spread the word, y'all, Christ is born.
The devil's rule over earth now is soon gone,

So let the myrrh, frankinsence burn, y'all been warned
Two thousand years ago, now the angels sound the horn.
No crown of thorns. Bow down, praise Him.
New guard floatin' out, but my style's amazin'.

Do-re-fo-sol-la-ti-do, my army suit's my tuxedo.
I'm a ghetto prophet to my people,
A ghetto priest, Adonis, criminal mind, but at
Least I'm honest, so I seek what the Savior promised.

Then I climb where I can stand the highest, so I can
Tell it to every man, woman and child, what the time is.
We sending this to all nations. The birth of
Christ calls for a celebration, yeah.

FIX ME JESUS

Traditional
Arranged by RAPHAEL SAADIQ,
TAURA STINSON and H. DOOBIE POWELL

*Recorded a half step lower.

JESUS IS ON THE MAINLINE

Traditional
Arranged by RAPHAEL SAADIQ
and TAURA STINSON

*In bass clef, x-noteheads denote foot stomps.

tell Him what ____ you want. ____
tell Him what ____ you want.) ____

Spoken: (see additional lyrics I)   (Call Him.)

(Call Him.)   (Call Him.)

(Call Him.)

* In treble clef, x-noteheads denote handclaps..

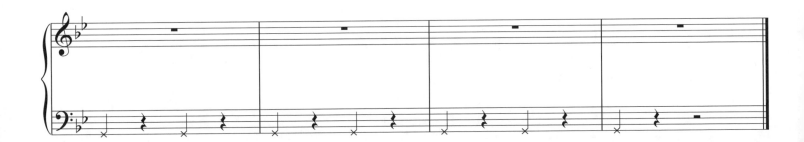

Additional lyrics 1

Go on and tell Jesus,

In your time of crisis, when the hour is late and the rent is due,
When you think there's nothing more that you can do, I want you all to let God's love fill you.
Now remember, God's love is overflowing, a love for all mankind,

No matter where they live, what they look like, or who they love.
Whether we approve of their actions or disapprove, we love them

Because God loves them. Now this love is not easy: over the years we build up hardness in our hearts
From old heartbreaks and disappointments and prejudices and times when we choose

Not to forgive. It starts when we're young, and by the time you get to be my age
You can have a hard, crusty buildup around your heart. I want you all to ask Jesus

To melt the hardness in your hearts, to wash you clean and let you love again.
Sister Aretha, could you sing that one more time for me please?

Additional lyrics II

Practice love on your children.

Love your parents, love your neighbors,
And pretty soon the hardness will melt, and you will be able to love even your enemies,
For love is the most creative power in the universe. Love is
God; God is...

Thank you, Jesus...
My baby girl is here.
Praise Jesus.
Thank you, Father.
Thank you.

AS

Words and Music by
STEVIE WONDER

Moderately

Did you know that true love asks for noth - ing?

Her ac - cept - ance is the way we pay.

Did you know that life has giv - en love a guar - an - tee to last

Recorded a half step lower.